BEATING TEACHER BURNOUT

How to Maintain Your Well-Being in One of the Toughest &
Most Emotionally Consuming Careers

Leana Anthony-Spence

Published in the United Kingdom

First Printing Edition, 2023

Table of Contents

Beating Teacher Burnout: How to Maintain Your Well-Being in One of the Toughest & Most Emotionally Consuming Careers

Part I: Understanding the Problem

Part II: Tackling the Problem

Part III: Maintaining Your New Work-Life Balance

INTRODUCTION

"The best teachers are those who show you where to look but don't tell you what to see."

~ Alexandra K. Trenfor

Teaching is, in my opinion, one of the greatest professions on the face of the earth. From their foundational years and beyond, children rely on teachers to help them navigate the world of learning. In most cases, this includes everything from developing social-emotional skills all the way through to exploring the sciences that stand as the precursor to medical professions. Teachers are the helm of shaping tomorrow's critical thinkers and problem-solvers and, yet, they often get the short end of the stick.

Despite the fact that schools are a much-needed building block of society, teachers are seen as dispensable and provided with little to no support in their careers. As someone who has been in this industry for 16 years, bearing witness to the number of amazing teachers that we are losing to this huge lack of support is incredibly concerning. These are life-changers and the shapers of little minds who are walking out the proverbial door on teaching and never looking back.

For those who will read this and claim that this is a generational issue, let me assure you that it isn't.

How so?

Well, because I've witnessed both fledgling teachers and seasoned pros leave this industry. And you don't have to look very far to find evidence of this. All you have to do is turn on the TV, scroll through social media, or listen to the radio and you'll be inundated with stories of teacher strikes and the grievances that they are trying to bring everyone's attention to. I can tell you one thing for free: these grievances are felt by teachers across all levels of experience.

In this guide, I want to provide teachers – novices and pros alike – with the tools that they will need to navigate the new landscape of teaching. The question I'm sure you're asking at this point is...why listen to me?

That's a good question and here's the honest answer. I've been through the spectrum of roles in education over the last (almost) two decades. I've had several roles, such as Head of Department, early career mentor, induction tutor, pastoral wellbeing facilitator, and science teacher in that time. I've worked in several types of educational facilities, including inner-city comprehensive schools. To cut a long story short, I've seen practically every facet of the school system.

But I'm not just an educator. I'm also a mum of two.

What pains me are the potentially damaging ramifications of the great (teacher's) resignation. Will my children have inspiring, caring, and compassionate teachers a year or two from now? Will our teachers miss out on the opportunity to watch their abilities in action through the progress of the children they teach?

I know that this system of dysfunction can be turned around and, in the meantime, I want to share my top tips for avoiding burnout and helping you cope with the rigour of teaching. Although there are definitely issues in areas of administration and where salaries are concerned, there are a few other issues that I see as solvable problems, which we can tackle right now.

Before that, let's look at who this guide is for.

Who is this Guide For?

Well, you've probably already guessed that this isn't a guide for plumbers. Jokes aside, this guide is for anyone who is looking for a sign of whether to stay or leave the profession. It's for anyone who is worn out and desperately searching for answers. It is for the teacher who spends far too much of her own money on her lessons, classroom, and students but feels like she can't get a break. It is for the teacher who cries himself to sleep at night, wondering what on earth he was thinking when he picked this as a career. It is for all of us – all of us whose spark is teaching and who just need a little help to be reminded of the fact.

What Will You Learn?

I'm passionate about teaching, but I know firsthand that to have a long-term career, you have to adopt strategies to look after yourself. In this guide, I'm going to walk you through the effects of this career on your mental health as well as how you can combat those effects. We'll look at everything from setting yourself up for a great day to becoming more proactive in a reactive environment, building better relationships, identifying the signs of stress and burnout, and prioritizing your health in this fast-paced industry.

Ultimately, you're going to learn how to put yourself first, how to move through stressful situations without allowing them to alter your emotional state, and how to enjoy your career.

LEANA ANTHONY-SPENCE

Beating Teacher Burnout: How to Maintain Your Well-Being in One of the Toughest & Most Emotionally Consuming Careers

Part I: Understanding the Problem

CHAPTER 1 – TEACHERS FORM THE BEDROCK OF SOCIETY

A s the pandemic rolled around in 2020 and parents were tasked with "teaching" their children from home, there was something that they very soon realised: this job isn't easy! What's more, is that the average parent had anywhere between 1 and 4 children to "teach". Plus, these were their own children! As teachers, we have to get to know perfect strangers – young humans who have thoughts and ideas of their own and who all come from different backgrounds and upbringings. To top it off, we're dealing with the emotions and egos of a classroom full of children. That's roughly 30 young minds that we have to stimulate and drive a love (or at least an understanding) of a subject into.

These people couldn't even handle 1-4 of their own children!

I laugh when I think about this, but the fact is that pre-covid, our careers weren't seen as important kinks in the societal chain. In fact, teaching was seen as easy. After all, all we have to do is show up and talk to a bunch of children for a couple of hours and go home. Plus, we get all of those "holidays". This is where the quotation marks around the word "teaching" is going to come in. Many people thought that teaching was easy because this is the view that they had of the industry. Moreover, they had no idea what really goes into teaching – things like:

- Prep work;

- Lesson plans;
- Training to be more trauma-informed;
- Training to be more special needs informed;
- Seminars that eat into our lunch hours and downtime;
- Money that we often spend on our own supplies;
- Additional administrative tasks that many of us deal with in the week after the "holidays" kick-off and a week before they end;
- Salaries that get spread out over the 12 months of the year when, in many cases, we're not being covered for the "holiday" months;
- And much more.

So, yes. I say that parents had to "teach" their children and place the word in quotation marks because all they had to handle was an intense amount of homework.

Now, I want to clear something up. I am a parent too and I am in no way saying that all parents regard teachers in this manner, but the general consensus – pre-covid – was that teachers have it easy. While the pandemic was an undeniably unfortunate time for countless people around the world, I take the tiniest piece of solace in knowing that the role of teachers is beginning to come to light as something valuable, even fundamental, to the very fabric of our societies.

The real conundrum is why teachers are still walking away from the field. One of the reasons is that people just don't see how important this job is. That feeling of not mattering in the grand scheme of things can weigh heavily on top of the existing stress that teachers face.

So, I'm going to help you understand why your job matters.

Chapter 1

Why Your Job as Teacher Matters

Teachers across the UK have been demanding that their needs be met and, yet, the Government has continued to offer lower than expected pay-rises amidst a burgeoning level of inflation. I understand that the importance of a role is subjective to some, but at the bare bones of the matter, teachers provide a resource that is second to none. We create engineers, doctors, future leaders, ballet dancers, artists, singers, scientists, and everyone else in between. Without schools and, therefore, teachers, all of that ceases to exist.

And I know that there are those who will argue semantics with me, so I'll humour them now.

Here's an answer for the person who will ask, "What did we do before there were schools?"

We had "villages". Some people worked, others cooked, others cleaned, others watched over the children, others sewed clothes...I could keep going, but you get the picture. For some of you, this might sound like a dream, but for others, this might sound like a nightmare.

Then there are those who will ask, "Why can't we just have our children sitting at home and learning remotely?"

That is possible. There are parents who homeschool their children, but they are also very hands-on parents. In most cases, one or more parents work in the home and are responsible for administering the homeschool curriculum. The person teaching them through their TV or computer monitor is there to substantiate what their parent is already teaching them. These parents have to enrol their children in clubs and sports to ensure socialisation and they are with their children 24/7. Again – a dream for some and a nightmare for others.

Schools are necessary because they play a specific role in modern-day society. No, they are not glorified daycare centres. They facilitate camaraderie through group projects and activities. They teach children the discipline necessary for this world by having them wake up at specific times and follow a routine every day. And, yes, they provide parents with a place to leave their children that is far better – in many cases – than the home they leave behind every morning. It is a safe haven for some children and – as can be seen through the issue of food security amongst children who had to stay home during the pandemic – schools also provide the fulfilment of basic needs for some children.

You, as a teacher, know that this role is important and you know that (subconsciously) everyone else knows it too. Even if we all went remote again, we would still need teachers to plan lessons around specific curriculums and provide support to children and parents in a remote fashion.

At the end of the day, this career matters.

You are fulfilling a vital role.

I don't think I need to go on and remind you of all of the problems that you're already faced with in your career, so let's move on to the effects that this undervaluing is having on your mental health.

CHAPTER 2 – THE EFFECTS ON TEACHERS' MENTAL HEALTH

There is one harsh reality of this career path that will not go away: the lack of support and undervaluing of our roles have a profound impact on our mental health. I've been told a number of times that I'm a rare species for handling my career in the manner that I have, but that doesn't mean that I haven't had my fair share of struggles in this industry. Witnessing teachers – friends – that I respected in the industry crumble under the massive weight that they were shouldering is nothing short of heartbreaking. Seeing the difficulties that teachers face in the early stages of their careers has made me wonder whether there is hope for this vital piece of our social puzzle.

So, to answer the question that I'm sure many of you are thinking, yes, I have had my doubts before. However, they were fleeting and only momentary because I made a conscious decision to stay in this industry and to find what worked best for me and my mental health. You could, even after reading this, still decide to leave this career behind for good. That's alright. It doesn't make you any less valuable and it certainly doesn't make you weak.

But I believe that you owe it to yourself to give this a real shot with tools that can help you make the most of a tough career.

Before I get ahead of myself, let's look at the ways in which the lack of support affects your mental health.

Lack of Support

Human beings are pack animals. Somewhere along a river bank, a long time ago, a crocodile ate one of our babies and we decided that we were better off in the safety of numbers. This is where that "village", which we looked at earlier, was born. When you have a lack of support in your field, it can take a toll on your mental and physical health. Heading off to work in the morning can feel like you're being made to walk the plank.

We have administrators that tell us how to do our jobs and superintendents who believe that, somehow, everything is always our fault. While this isn't something that occurs across the board, it happens frequently enough, and in a widespread manner enough, to make teachers tuck tail and leg it straight out of the field.

A small shift in how you see your workday can have a tremendously positive impact on how the lack of support at work affects you. For one, seeing your career as just that – a small part of your life and not the be-all and end-all of your life – will allow you to let go of certain slights. Being able to switch between your work brain and your life brain will help you do this. I'll elaborate on how this is done in Chapter 6.

What you should know right now is that this lack of support, as well as the ballooning workload that you're expected to take on, will have you on the verge of burnout if you don't do something about it. Just know that you're not alone and that you can overcome the effects of this career choice. There are countless teachers who feel the way you do. As a matter of fact, studies by the National Association of Schoolmasters Union of Women Teachers have shown that 27% of teachers are reporting signs of burnout while a staggering 91% have reported that their job is adversely affecting their mental health. [1]

Clearly, something is very wrong here, but now that you know that you're not alone in this, you can begin planning your way forward.

Part II: Tackling the Problem

CHAPTER 3 – SETTING YOURSELF UP FOR A GREAT DAY

O nce you've understood that there are deep-rooted issues in the education sphere and that you're not alone, you can make the call to stay or leave your career behind. I hope that I've convinced you of the importance of your role in society and that you'll decide to stay. If that is the direction that you're leaning in, let's begin with the first tool in your arsenal: setting yourself up for a great day.

Many teachers who are in the early days of their careers walk into their newfound jobs without being fully prepared for the ride they will go through. Nipping that lack of preparation in the bud by creating a template for a great day will alleviate a great deal of mental strain.

As such, you need to prepare for your great day the night before.

A Good Bedtime Routine

A great day is set up the night before. In other words, what you do before bedtime tonight will have an impact on your day tomorrow. Professionals in high-powered roles have known this for decades. Now, it's time for you to see yourself as the high-powered professional that you are and take ownership of your role. So, let's look at the basic premise of a great bedtime routine.

1. **Avoid using any backlit devices before bed.** In the two hours leading up to bedtime, avoid using your devices. This includes phones, tablets, laptops, and TVs. I know – shock horror! How dare I suggest that you put away your precious distraction devices? The thought of it! The fact is that these devices trick your pineal gland (the gland in your brain that's responsible for producing your sleep hormones) into thinking it's daytime. A pineal gland that thinks its daytime will stop producing the hormones needed for you to achieve deep and restful sleep, such as melatonin. Don't worry, you'll get used to it. You could read a book or journal your thoughts. If you're dealing with a great deal of anxiety at night, try something a bit more mentally draining like a puzzle or some sort of fidget activity.

2. **Make sure your room is cool and dark before bed.** Give hot baths and showers before bed the boot and opt for lukewarm water instead. You need to keep your body and your bedroom at a consistently cool temperature in order to fall into a deep sleep with minimal sleep disturbances. Darkness is your pineal gland's friend, so make sure your room is dark enough to allow this gland to do its job.

3. **Do some of your morning tasks in the evening.** If there is anything that you need to get done in the morning, which can be done in the evening, get it over and done with. This includes things such as picking your outfit for the next day and making sure any tins, lunch boxes, and water bottles that you'll need for the day are washed. If you can prep most of the food that you'll be taking for lunch in the evening,

please do that. This will give you time to yourself in the morning and you'll feel prepared to take on the day.

Now, let's turn our focus to your mornings.

A Great Morning Routine

What does a great morning routine look like? Well, it starts with some "me time". If possible, wake up an hour earlier each morning. Yes, this would mean getting to bed an hour earlier too, but it is so worth it. Waking up to the silence of the early morning hours will provide you with a stillness of mind and spirit that is hard to match. This is especially important if you live with a roommate, a partner, a spouse, or children. The chaos of the morning is often felt through the energy of the most stressed person in the room. If that's you, you need that extra hour to mentally prepare yourself for the day ahead. You could try:

1. **Waking up ten minutes earlier than normal.** If waking up a whole hour earlier than normal sounds like your idea of torture, you could do it gradually. Every night, get to bed 10 minutes earlier than normal and set your alarm for 10 minutes earlier than you would usually wake up. After a week, add another 10 minutes. Keep doing this each week until you reach your goal of waking up an hour earlier.

2. **Find something that you can enjoy doing every morning.** This could be practising yoga, going for a run, doing some light stretching, meditating, or anything else that will benefit your health. Spend at least 20 minutes on this every morning.

3. **Prioritize eating a healthy meal.** Intermittent fasting works wonders for many people but not so much for women who have hormonal imbalances such as PCOS, hypo- or hyperthyroidism, or adrenal issues. Women going through menopause also need to take stock of what and when they are eating in order to support their natural decreases in progesterone and estrogen.

4. **Plan your day.** Create a checklist in order of priority of what you need to do that day. Make sure this covers everything from work and personal perspectives, but don't forget to be flexible. If you're hyper-focused on crossing things off your checklist, it could cause you anxiety – especially if you're unable to complete one or more tasks on the checklist.

This is all a part of becoming more proactive – something that we'll explore further in the next chapter.

CHAPTER 4 – BECOMING PROACTIVE IN A REACTIVE INDUSTRY

O nce you've set yourself up for a great day, you need to take your planning to the next level by getting down to the microscopic details of your schedule. Time management is essential and while you don't want to feel like you're filling every second of your day with being busy, you do want to ensure that you're maximizing the time that you have. Feeling overwhelmed and as if there is just no time in the day is one of the many reasons why a third of teachers who qualified in England alone in the last decade have chosen to leave the profession. In 2021 alone, 81,000 teachers (of the 270,000 who qualified between 2011 and 2020) walked away from teaching for good. [2]

With this in mind, let's explore how planning can make you more proactive.

Planning Makes You Proactive

When you block out your time effectively, you'll be more prepared for the times when life hands you lemons. If, for example, you know that you have lesson planning, assignment creation, test creation, marking, and other tasks, such as filing, you need to set aside days for those tasks.

When you dedicate specific days to your various tasks, it's easier to stay on track. More importantly, when you don't have a million things to attend to in one day, you won't be caught unawares by the slightest wave that threatens to rock your schedule.

Classroom Management will Lighten the Load

It is really true that the children who exhibit the worst outwardly behaviour are the ones who need the most compassion. However, that doesn't mean that you need to let erratic behaviour run your classroom. Over the years, I have cultivated a set of behaviour and classroom management tools that work with almost 100% efficacy. Now, I'm going to share a few of the best ones with you.

Before you can dream of managing your classroom or the behaviour of the children in it, you need to take a long, hard look at yourself. Are you a robot? Are you made of steel? Are you superhuman?

No, you aren't. You need to give yourself some slack and realise that you are just a human being. There are some things that you can't fix, so please be kind to yourself. Teaching is an incredibly emotional game. You're not dealing with figures on a screen or products in a shop. These are human beings with their own emotions, thoughts, and ideas. Moreover, children of all ages have massive energy and all of those swirling energies are bound to clash from time to time. Pace yourself and try not to swing too far in either direction where emotions are concerned.

Equally important is remembering that things don't always go according to plan. You could have planned the perfect lesson differentiated for all special education needs, had the healthiest meal before school, and arrived on site feeling fresh and fabulous, only for it all to fall apart due to the energy in the room that morning. You know the saying, "It's not you, it's me"? Well, this is the reverse. Sometimes, the non-desirable behaviours exhibited by our students can be for reasons completely out of your control or can be led by emotion. One thing is for certain, good behaviour management is essential because low-level disruption affects the environment and learning. Speaking of which, let's dive deeper into behaviour management now.

Understanding Behaviour in the Classroom

Knowing that your students are watching you at all times is the first step that you need to take in terms of understanding behaviour in the classroom. As teachers, you set the tone and the culture for how your children will behave. If you're walking around the school with a scowl on your face and a temperament that says, "do not approach me", your students will develop the same attitude. Similarly, walking around school with an air of positivity will spread positivity amongst your students.

It's all about modelling the behaviour that you want them to embody.

If you're thinking to yourself that this isn't something that you should have to do, then you're missing the whole point. When you walk up to a cashier, you expect to be greeted with a smile no matter how much of a pain in the butt the last customer was. You are being paid to be at school – and probably more than that cashier. It isn't your home. So, just as much as you need to learn to leave work at work, you need to learn to leave home at home. If you don't, you're going to have a miserable time in both spheres of your life.

As such, I always recommend that you model simple courtesies, such as:

- Always saying "please" and "thank you".
- Greeting other teachers and students in the corridors.
- Holding the door open for another teacher or student.
- Smiling and generally being friendly.

Manners maketh the human!

Again, you're not superhuman. You might be going through an incredibly difficult time at home. You might have just lost someone dear to you or finances might be weighing heavily on your mind. I understand this, trust me. I also understand that some children are more difficult than others, but if you try to build positive relationships with your colleagues and students – albeit within the confines of your professional boundaries – you will notice the difference.

Other than what we've already explored, have a look at the top behaviour management tips that I recommend:

- **Be the boss.** Your students should know that you are in charge and there should be clear boundaries. This will make them feel safe and they will know, with certainty, where they stand with you.
- **Use positive language.** There are going to be days when you talk to your maker – whoever you believe that is – and ask them for the grace to not scream at the top of your lungs. These are the boundary-pushing days and the days when positive language is needed the most. Instead of focusing on the 2 children who aren't doing what you've asked them to do, focus on the 28 who are. You could say

something along the lines of, "A little over 90% of us are ready to get started. We're just waiting for the last 3 to join us."

- **Use the sandwich method.** When addressing concerning behaviour, it's best to use the sandwich method. This involves starting with a positive, addressing the concern, and ending with a positive. It will have a great on the outcome of the interaction.

- **Praise good behaviour.** Becoming more attuned to looking for good behaviour as opposed to looking for concerning behaviour is always going to be a good idea. When you're constantly harping on about the negative, it will hardwire both your and your students' brains for negativity.

- **Create law and order.** Other than boundaries, you also want to set a routine as early as possible. Nobody likes chaos and students definitely do not like a chaotic classroom. Children like to know what to expect and any uncertainty leaves too much room for fear and anxiety to breed. Set simple rules on behaviour and a few non-negotiables. One of mine is that they are not allowed to speak while I am speaking.

- **Give clear instructions.** You cannot expect children to guess what they're supposed to do or how they're supposed to behave in your class. Be precise. You can say something along the lines of, "I'm expecting everyone to have their pens down, mouths closed, and eyes on the board."

- **Be flexible.** It's important to get to know your students' special education needs (SEN) or English as an additional language (EAL) needs. Reset your expectations accordingly and express this.

Ultimately, you have to get control of your class and the behaviours that are bound to be exhibited at some point or the next. You're not preaching to a room full of statues, after all. Now, let's get into the topic that many teachers dread – and not just the novices!

Dealing with Conflict or Disciplinary Matters

I'm a proponent of the firm but fair approach to discipline. Children are sponges and they want to know that they are not being treated unfairly or that the next person isn't more special than them in some way. Therefore, if you treat your students differently or take an unfair approach in any circumstance, they are going to pick up on that. They might accept their punishment – albeit begrudgingly – but they will never let that moment go. They will hold onto that memory and you will, most likely, never rebuild the trust that has been broken.

To avoid inflating a situation or having a student feel embarrassed over something that could very well be a misunderstanding, have conversations around behaviour correction in private. Children (especially when they enter their tween and teen years) are incredibly concerned with their image. If you're going to do anything to hamper that image, they are going to rise to the challenge of preserving that image. You have no idea how many children have massive egos in front of their friends but will shed a tear and explain what they are going through in private. I've seen this happen dozens of times – if not, more.

This is why working on relationship building is so crucial to your success as a teacher – and when I say success, I mean having a peaceful and enjoyable time at work that benefits both you and your students. Nonetheless, conflicts will arise every so often and when it does, the relationship between you and one of your students can break down. One of my favourite openers with a student in this situation is, " You are making it really difficult for us to have a good relationship." Students often look at me confused while they think about what I said to them. It puts an element of control into their lap and they think about how they are contributing negatively. Students need to learn to take ownership of their behaviour and the consequences.

Doling out more punishment isn't going to lead to better behaviour, nor will it ensure that new, positive behaviours are learnt. As a restorative justice facilitator, I always resolve conflict in the following manner which is powerful when used correctly:

- What had happened? (Establishing the nature of the conflict.)
- What were you thinking/feeling? (What might have led to the conflict.)
- Who has been affected? (Who was involved and what was the extent of the damage.)
- What do you think you could do to make the situation better? (Is there any reconciliation that can help to resolve the situation and how can this be facilitated.)

Getting Organised & Addressing Peer Pressure

Earlier, I mentioned that lesson plans don't always go according to – well – the plan. However, you still need to be organised. Have your lessons planned and prepped before they begin and you will be able to focus on administering the lesson and managing the classroom – two things that are already like full-time jobs on their own!

You can then work on setting group norms and allowing the power of the crowd to positively influence the students who tend to be more difficult to deal with. Having something that is "your thing" with your students can drive that sense of unity that becomes incredibly protective over defending the norm. It might sound like you're creating a band of minions, but it works! Whether it's a secret handshake, a ritual or mantra that you begin class with, or anything else that falls within your professional boundaries, go for it!

In the long run, they will "police" themselves and encourage good behaviour amongst one another and that is the type of positive influence we want to see in the classroom.

CHAPTER 5 – BUILDING BETTER RELATIONSHIPS

R elationships matter. It doesn't matter how you look at it or where you are in the world, relationships are at the root of every facet of our lives. Whether it's the relationship you have with your local barista or the relationship you have with yourself, they're all important. As a teacher, however, you're going to want to pay more attention to the following relationships.

The Relationship with Your Students

As previously mentioned, building a relationship with your students – no matter how old or young they are – is one of the key steps to having a more pleasant experience as a teacher. You're going to be with these children for a good portion of your day. While other stresses of the job will impact your experience as a teacher, having a disengaged or difficult group is going to make it all feel a thousand times worse.

Keep in mind that this is something that you're going to have to do every single year. The good news is that if you're really invested in your career and in your relationship with your students, taking this step won't feel as daunting as people make it out to be.

So, how do you build a relationship with your students?

You start by developing a genuine interest in what they like. If you have students that are of the age where they can clearly communicate their likes and dislikes, you already have the upper hand. By simply opening up the lines of communication with them and allowing them to express themselves outside of the anxieties and expectations of the school "system", you give them the sense of comfort that they need to trust you. And trust, if you did not already know this, is crucial for getting young ears to perk up when you speak.

Other than this, exhibiting kindness and forgiveness will win them over. When your students feel as though they can make mistakes in your presence, they will be more open to learning. It will drive their curiosity because they won't be wondering if and when you'll come down on their heads for inconsequential slip-ups. Having a sound and respectful relationship with your students cannot be underestimated.

Then there is the relationship with yourself.

The Relationship with Yourself

There is no one on the face of this earth (*whether you believe it's God's green earth or mother earth or a product of some random chemical reaction*) who is going to be with you for as long as you are going to be with yourself. If you don't like the person looking back at you in the mirror, guess what? You have a long way to go with that person.

I'm not saying that there aren't things that you can decide you dislike, nor am I saying that you can't be compassionately critical of the flaws that you have the power to change. However, what I am saying is that you need to either change the parts of yourself that do not serve you or learn to embrace every part of yourself. It usually works out as being a little bit of both, but you have to decide how you want to approach the relationship.

Some of the ways in which you can develop a deeper relationship with yourself include:

- Picking a new hobby and enjoying your own company.
- Blocking out time for your self-care every week.
- Using positive affirmations to remind yourself that you are human, whole as you are, and worthy of good things.
- Embracing your flaws and celebrating who you are.
- Thinking about what your strengths are and playing to them.
- Seeing setbacks as opportunities to learn and not as failures.

When you have a better relationship with yourself and your students, life's stresses will have less of a negative impact on your outlook. That being said, it would also do you some good to look toward someone who has been in the industry longer than you have for support.

Your Relationship With A Mentor

Finding a mentor is something that everyone across every industry should consider, especially if the industry in question is as mentally and physically demanding as teaching.

A mentor can become your voice of reason in difficult situations. They can advise you on how to traverse conflict with your superiors and your colleagues. They've also been where you've been and can give you that extra bit of reassurance that you will pull through.

Of course, this means that your mentor needs to be someone in the teaching or education sphere. I should make it clear that your mentor should have more experience in the industry than you, but that doesn't mean that they have to be older than you. If, like me, you retrained to be a teacher further along the curve of your career trajectory, you may very well find that there are few teachers who are younger than you and are willing to mentor you. A good mentor should be someone who:

- Has a positive outlook on life.
- Is willing to watch your career from a distance and offer you advice.
- Will help you reach your goals.
- Has the necessary experience to keep you motivated when you encounter obstacles.

Of course, there will be other defining factors that relate to your particular needs, but these are the general boxes that a mentor should tick. At this stage, you can begin looking at maintaining your new work-life balance.

Part III: Maintaining Your New Work-Life Balance

CHAPTER 6 – PRIORITIZING YOUR MENTAL HEALTH

Your mental health will take a toll on your physical health if you're not careful. A constant state of stress will mean that there is more cortisol in your bloodstream [4] and this can lead to:

- Increased chronic inflammation.
- Elevated blood glucose levels.
- A weakened immune system.
- Elevated blood pressure.
- Weakened liver and pancreatic function.

Before all of this comes to a head, your body will start screaming for help and these pleas will manifest themselves as the early signs of burnout.

The Signs of Teacher Burnout

Burnout is a tricky beast to peg down to just one symptom and one intensity because it is subjective to our individual tolerances for stress and how we manage stress. People have often told me that I'm built differently and asked me how I haven't buckled under the pressure yet. There are many reasons why some people can navigate more stress than others, but those reasons aren't important. This isn't a game of who can wear their stress like a badge of honour better. What is important to know is that just because your teacher friends aren't experiencing burnout under the same conditions that you're subjected to, that doesn't mean you won't. Equally, just because you're standing strong in a storm, that doesn't mean the winds of stress aren't battering your colleagues.

With that said, let's look at some of the common signs of burnout:

- **Fatigue/Exhaustion**. This is not the same thing as just being tired. The fatigue that comes with burnout will hit you like a steam train. You will not have the energy to make it through the day. Just getting out of bed will feel like pulling teeth. This is often accompanied by a low mood. So, if you're tired but upbeat, it is not burnout fatigue.
- **Detachment**. Where teaching is concerned, this might include a detachment from your job. You might come in to work and drag your feet through the day. Your detachment might have you experiencing brain fog that interferes with your ability to teach.
- **Affected/Reduced Work Performance**. Getting through the simplest of tasks might be too much for you to bear. Procrastination will become the norm as well as a surge in irritability towards your students. Ultimately, you'll feel apathetic towards everyone and everything related to your job and it will show.

If you find that you're in a constant state of stress, anxiety, or panic, these could be the precursors to burnout. We don't often pay attention to these subtle signs because they're not "killing us". At least we think that they aren't. However, studies have shown that stress-related chronic illnesses are on the rise. So, actually, these things can kill you.

Before your anxiety spirals out of control, you might notice that you're experiencing imposter syndrome or being weighed down by the need for perfection. As you become more on edge at work, you'll question whether the colleagues that you're on friendly terms with really are as friendly as they seem. In a nutshell, you begin to go – well – a little nutty. Stress makes you alert. It's there to keep you safe from harm but, in a world where there aren't any crocodiles or sabre-toothed tigers waiting to eat you, your stress response starts making everything around you feel like a threat.

If you're feeling anxious and uneasy all day long, this is the first sign that you're on a slippery slope to burnout. Pay attention to it. When you do, you'll be able to identify your stress and prevent it from developing into burnout.

How to Curb Burnout

A little earlier in the guide, we looked at self-care as a means to combat stress and we're going to look at this in more detail now. Your self-care routine is going to look different when compared to the self-care routines of those around you. Even if you were an identical twin, your self-care routine would not be exactly the same as your sibling's.

To put it plainly, you're going to have to determine what self-care means to you. I'll provide you with a few suggestions below, but you'll need to establish your own self-care routine.

Self-care can look like:

- Staying home when you've been asked to go out or going out with friends when all you want to do is stay home.
- Indulging in bubble baths.
- Engaging in meditation sessions.
- Going for a run by yourself or taking up an exercise class.

- Eating healthy and staying hydrated.
- Splurging on your favourite skincare products.
- Setting clear boundaries and honouring yourself.

You might already be implementing some of these self-care practices. If you are, great! If you feel like you need to focus on other areas of your personal care, then go for it. Sometimes, it's not so much how much self-care we're practising that makes the difference, but the type of self-care.

With a good self-care routine place, focus on purging anything from your life that doesn't align with your mental well-being. Conversations that drain you of your energy and relationships that feel toxic to you need to be done away with. If you don't do this, their energy will continue to deplete your mental reserves and worsen your feelings of dread, despair, and anxiety.

Seek out the support of people who love you, including your friends and family members. The more stressed you become, the more tempting it will feel to just shut people out – including those who mean well. Push yourself to connect with people who care about you. Isolating yourself will only lead to feelings of loneliness and it will make you question whether people truly care about you when it is you, in fact, who is actively cutting them off.

Finally, learning to set boundaries will definitely free up some of your mental reserves. While it's easier to set firm boundaries from the get-go, you can still work on setting boundaries if you've been in a position for a few months or even years. It's imperative that you establish a work-life balance because, without it, you'll reach burnout levels at lightning speed. Healthy boundaries include:

- Create a definitive time for marking papers and assignments.
- Have specific times for helping students or speaking with them.
- Keep your personal contact number private and communicate with parents via your administrator, a classroom app, or email. Giving parents your phone number gives them far too much power to contact you in your personal time.
- Do not attend to work emails or calls after hours or on weekends. All emergencies should go via a school director, headmaster, headmistress, or administrator.
- Learn to leave work at work. If you can't fix it right now, don't focus on it in your personal time. When you're back at work, give the issue your full attention. When you're off the clock, force yourself to put it out of your mind.

Now that you have your mental health prioritized, let's look at the ways in which you can prioritize your physical health. After all, it's all connected!

CHAPTER 7 – PRIORITIZING YOUR PHYSICAL HEALTH

Y our physical health and mental health are interconnected – there is no denying that fact. If you take care of your mental health, your physical health will flourish. If you take care of your physical health, it can support your mental health. As such, it's crucial that you start looking at your physical health. It doesn't matter how young or old you believe you are. If you're not taking care of your body, it is not going to be able to take care of you.

Plus, you only have this one body. Sure, we can get spare parts for our bodies now, but it's not like you can trade it in for a newer model.

Jokes aside, let's wrap up your guide to beating teacher burnout with tips on how to maintain your physical well-being.

Getting Back to Basics

If you're struggling to maintain the basics, this is a good sign that you're hanging on by a very thin thread. What are the basics? These are things such as personal hygiene and having the time to eat well. You are not a robot. Your life is defined by more than just your job. You have to practice these basic elements of self-care or you're going to lose your sense of self-worth and work yourself to the bone.

Prioritize eating healthy food and keeping well hydrated every day of your life. Eating a nutritious meal isn't just an act of self-love, it's an act of self-preservation. If you didn't already know this, your gut is filled with billions of microorganisms that run a delicate balance of the ecosystem that is your body. Yes, all of that gut flora is responsible for every aspect of your well-being – from mood calibration to immune functioning.

Fueling your body with a nutritious, high-fibre diet is going to work wonders for your health. The major plus is that, once your gut flora is balanced, those tiny microorganisms will help combat the effects of a stressful work environment. While you should do your part to find a diet that works with your personal physique, I can recommend including the following:

- Cruciferous vegetables;
- Fruit;
- Wholegrain pasta;
- Brown rice;
- Wholegrain cereal;
- Nuts and legumes.

Try your best to keep away from high-sugar food items and highly processed goods. These are often fast-releasing (meaning that they provide you with a spike of energy before you crash) and they contain synthetic materials that your body struggles to break down. This can lead to chronic inflammation, poor gut flora, and a slew of resultant health issues.

So, here's my advice on eating well. If you can, take the time to prep your meals the night before. Then, actually sit down and eat your meal at school. Don't fill your break periods with more work. You need to be seated and chew your food thoroughly to avoid indigestion and possible long-term side effects of continual indigestion, which can include chronic reflux disease, hiatal hernias, and more.

Eating well and enjoying the food you eat play a significant role in your well-being. One of the areas that it aids the most is in your hormone calibration.

Balancing Your Hormones

There are many elements that go into maintaining your physical health, some of which we looked at earlier. These are elements such as having a consistent sleep-wake cycle, eating well, and exercising. All of these practices also have an impact on your hormones and your hormones have an effect on your mental health.

If you're too stressed, your adrenal glands produce too much adrenaline and cortisol.

If there's too much cortisol in your body, it can affect melatonin production and ruin your sleep schedule.

If your sleep schedule is ruined, it can exacerbate your adrenal overload and lead to erratic swings in progesterone and estrogen.

I could keep going, but we might be here well into the new year by the time I'm done telling you about the chain reactions that could potentially occur between all 50+ hormones that you have in your body. And here's the scary part: if even one of those hormones gets thrown far enough out of balance, it has the potential to throw all of your other hormones out of whack along with it.

Your body is a well-oiled machine, but it is not meant to take a hammering from the lifestyles that we live as modern-day humans. For those of you who are on the cusp of perimenopause or have transitioned through menopause, you'll know that your hormones (even with hormone replacements) will never be the same again. The gradual decline in progesterone and estrogen means that you need to start taking care of your body through conscious lifestyle choices. This includes monitoring your sleep-wake cycle, doing your best to get your stress levels under control, and practising an exercise that helps you release other hormones that are in excess as well as tension.

Exercises that are great for your hormones and for relieving stress include:

- **Walking or Jogging.** This creates full-body stimulation as you have to coordinate your arms, legs, eyes, and everything else in between to get from Point A to Point B. Yes, you might get your 10,000 steps a day at school, but taking a slow, short walk after school will work wonders for you. This is mainly because it gives you time to focus on nothing else but walking and your health, programming your brain to engage in more self-care and self-love routines.
- **Yoga.** Yoga works on your lymphatic system, which is responsible for helping your body excrete waste and debris from your system. There are several schools of yoga. Make sure you try one that you feel would suit your current level of physical fitness before progressing to other modalities.
- **Mindfulness Meditation.** Becoming more mindful and present in the moment will help you to stop stressing about the past or potential future. A lot of our stress is rooted in things we wish we had done differently and anticipation of tasks that we will need to complete in the near or distant future. Find a mindfulness meditation routine that works for

you and try to practice it every morning. You will thank yourself for it later.

If you focus on taking care of yourself, everything else will fall into place. Remember, you are worth every act of self-care. You can be passionate about your career and still prioritize yourself above all else.

IN CLOSING

Teacher burnout is a very real problem that all teachers will have to face at some point in their lives. It is my goal to help teachers face this problem while it is in its emergent stages and not when it has become full-blown burnout. That way, we can avoid the detrimental effects that the stresses of teaching have on our teachers' mental health and we can retain these precious resources that are the very backbone of our social constructs.

If, at any point, you feel like your mental health is at risk, consult this guide and seek the help of a mental health professional. When you look back on your life, you'll realise that your career should have only been a fraction of it and that your health and happiness should always come first.

I wish you all the best of luck!

Thank you for reading.

REFERENCES & CITATIONS

1) NASUWT Team. (2023). ***Teacher Wellbeing Survey.*** https://www.nasuwt.org.uk/news/campaigns/teacher-wellbeing-survey.html

2) Pearce, T. (2023). ***UK schools sinking under teacher retention crisis and billions in funding cuts.*** WSWS. https://www.wsws.org/en/articles/2023/01/26/ocsr-j26.html

3) Ferlazzo, L. (2018). ***Building Relationships With Students Is the Most Important Thing a Teacher Can Do.*** Education Week. https://www.edweek.org/teaching-learning/opinion-response-building-relationships-with-students-is-the-most-important-thing-a-teacher-can-do/2018/10

4) Thau, L., et al. (2022). ***Physiology, Cortisol.*** National Library of Medicine. https://www.ncbi.nlm.nih.gov/books/NBK538239/#:~:text=Cortisol%20acts%20on%20the%20liver,gluconeogenesis%20and%20decrease%20glycogen%20synthesis.

Printed in Great Britain
by Amazon